Classic
Ballroom
Dances

FOR Peter al Jean

Charlie

Nov 18, 1992

By Charles Simic

TRANSLATIONS

ANTHOLOGY

CLASSIC BALLROOM DANCES

Poems by
Charles Simic

GEORGE BRAZILLER

New York

Some of these poems have previously appeared in the following
periodicals to whose editors grateful acknowledgment is made:
*Antaeus, Manassas Review, Field, The Virginia Quarterly Review,
The Iowa Review, The Mississippi Review, Durak, Pequod, Ironwood,
American Poetry Review, Seneca Review, The New England Review,
The Cornell Review, Quarterly West, Crazy Horse, The Georgia Review.*

"December Trees" (p. 50) and "Harsh Climate" (p. 54); © 1977
and 1979, respectively, by *The New Yorker Magazine, Inc.*

"Green Lampshade" (p. 25) and "Furniture Mover" (p. 40);
© December 1979, by *Poetry.*

The Author wishes to thank the National Endowment for the
Arts for the grant which helped him to complete this book.

Published in the United States in 1980 by George Braziller, Inc.
Copyright © 1980 by Charles Simic
All rights reserved.

For information address the publisher:
George Braziller, Inc.
One Park Avenue
New York, N.Y. 10016

Library of Congress Cataloging in Publication Data
Simic, Charles, 1938-
Classic ballroom dances.
(The Braziller series of poetry)
I. Title
PS3569.I4725C54   811'.54   80-14470
ISBN 0-8076-0973-0
ISBN 0-8076-0974-9 (pbk.)

Printed in the United States of America
First Edition

for HELEN

Contents

I

II

III

IV

I

THE TABLE OF DELECTABLE CONTENTS

*Of the genealogy and great antiquity
of the invisible.*

Why we can't see the end of our nose.

*The invisible's account of the way
in which it escaped from the visible.*

*How the invisible spends its time
when it rains.*

*How the invisible ate my grandfather
in a salad.*

*Of the first steps toward that vision
to which he aspired to the praise
of his jailers and executioners
and other excellent precepts.*

*The quaint comedy of the tongue
and the mouse trap.*

*Descartes saying to the invisible:
I am. I am.*

*Spinoza polishing a lens to gaze leisurely
into the depths of the invisible.*

*Of his life among the cockroaches,
and of what he saw and learned among
the ineffables.*

*The reckless act of opening and closing
of a door.*

*Of the great longing of the invisible
to see itself.*

*In sum, containing all manner of matters
of little import and lethal consequence.*

II

PRIMER

This kid got so dirty
Playing in the ashes.

When they called him home,
When they yelled his name over the ashes,

It was a lump of ashes
That answered.

Little lump of ashes, they said,
Here's another lump of ashes for dinner,

To make you sleepy,
And make you grow.

SCHOOL FOR DARK THOUGHTS

At daybreak,
Little one,
I can feel the immense weight
Of the books you carry.

Anonymous one,
I can hardly make you out
In that large crowd
On the frozen playground.

Simple one,
There are rulers and sponges
Along the whitewashed walls
Of the empty classroom.

There are windows
And blackboards,
One can only see through
With eyes closed.

EMPIRE OF DREAMS

On the first page of my dreambook
It's always evening
In an occupied country.
Hour before the curfew.
A small provincial city.
The houses all dark.
The store-fronts gutted.

I am on a street corner
Where I shouldn't be.
Alone and coatless
I have gone out to look
For a black dog who answers to my whistle.
I have a kind of halloween mask
Which I am afraid to put on.

ROLL CALL

Like entrees on a menu,
The way they call our names out one by one,
And Claudia steps forward chin up,
Promptly to disappear into thin air,

And her old father reluctant, fading
Before our eyes with something like
Equanimity. And Mrs. Murphy,
Transubstantiated, loosened from her human

Moorings. Once this much is grasped,
Life gets sweet, though we are hemmed in:
Bundles, suitcases, important-looking documents:
Shoving, lifting us off our feet . . .

A back parlor and there's a piano,
Allegedly, and a photographer.
Shadow of his hood on the wall
Next my dunce cap at a rakish angle.

GREAT INFIRMITIES

Everyone has only one leg.
So difficult to get around,
So difficult to climb the stairs
Without a cane or a crutch to our name.

And only one arm. Impossible contortions
Just to embrace the one you love,
To cut the bread on the table,
To put a coat on in a hurry.

I should mention that we are almost blind,
And a little deaf in both ears.
Perilous to be on the street
Among the congregations of the afflicted.

With only a few steps committed to memory,
Meekly we let ourselves be diverted
In the endless twilight—
Blind seeing-eye dogs on our leashes.

An immense stillness everywhere
With the trees always bare,
The raindrops coming down only halfway,
Coming so close and giving up.

BEGOTTEN OF THE SPLEEN

The Virgin Mother walked barefoot
among the land mines.
She carried an old man in her arms.
The dove on her shoulder

barked at the moon.
The earth was an old people's home.
Judas was the night nurse.
He kept emptying bedpans into river Jordan.

The old man had two stumps for legs.
He was on a dog-chain. St. Peter pushed a cart
loaded with flying carpets.
They weren't flying carpets.

They were bloody diapers.
It was a cock-fighting neighborhood.
The Magi stood on street corners
cleaning their nails with German bayonets.

The old man gave Mary Magdalena
a mirror. She lit a candle,
and hid in the outhouse. When she got thirsty,
she licked the mist off the glass.

That leaves Joseph. Poor Joseph.
He only had a cockroach
to load his bundles on.
Even when the lights came on she wouldn't run
into her hole.

And the lights came on:
The floodlights
in the guard towers.

PRODIGY

I grew up bent over
a chessboard.

I loved the word *endgame*.

All my cousins looked worried.

It was a small house
near a Roman graveyard.
Planes and tanks
shook its windowpanes.

A retired professor of astronomy
taught me how to play.

That must have been in 1944.

In the set we were using,
the paint had almost chipped off
the black pieces.

The white King was missing
and had to be substituted for.

I'm told but do not believe
that that summer I witnessed
men hung from telephone poles.

I remember my mother
blindfolding me a lot.

She had a way of tucking my head
suddenly under her overcoat.

In chess, too, the professor told me,
the masters play blindfolded,
the great ones on several boards
at the same time.

BABY PICTURES OF FAMOUS DICTATORS

The epoch of a streetcar drawn by horses;
The organ-grinder and his monkey.
Women with parasols. Little kids in rowboats
Photographed against a cardboard backdrop depicting
  an idyllic sunset
At the fairgrounds where they all went to see
The two-headed calf, the bearded
Fat lady who dances the dance of seven veils.

And the great famine raging through India . . .
Fortune-telling white rats pulling a card out of
  a shoebox
While Edison worries over the lightbulb,
And the first model of the sewing machine
Is delivered in a pushcart
To a modest white-fenced home in the suburbs,

Where there are always a couple of infants
Posing for the camera in their sailors' suits,
Out there in the garden overgrown with shrubs.
Lovable little mugs smiling faintly toward
The new century. Innocent. Why not?
All of them like ragdolls of the period
With those chubby porcelain heads
That shut their long eyelashes as you lay them down.

In a kind of perpetual summer twilight . . .
One can even make out the shadow of the tripod
  and the black hood
That must have been quivering in the breeze.
One assumes that they all stayed up late squinting
    at the stars,
And were carried off to bed by their mothers and big sisters,
While the dogs remained behind:
Pedigreed bitches pregnant with bloodhounds.

THE LITTLE TEAR-GLAND THAT SAYS

Then there was Johann,
The carousel horse—
except he wasn't really a carousel horse.

He grew up "in the naive realism
  of the Wolffian school,
which without close scrutiny regarded
logical necessity and reality as identical."

On Sundays, they took him
to the undertaker's for sugar.
All these people flying in their dreams,
he remarked.

He stood before the Great Dark Night of History,
a picture of innocence
held together by his mother's safety pins—
lissome, frisky.

Cool reflection soon showed
there were openings among the signatories
  of death certificates . . .
Plus those fine high leather boots that squeak . . .

On his exam he wrote:
The act of torture consists of various strategies
meant to increase
the imagination of the *homo sapiens*.

And then . . . the Viennese waltz.

TOY FACTORY

My mother is here,
And so is my father.

They work the night shift.
At the end of the assembly line,
They wind toys
To inspect their springs.

Here's a mechanical
Firing squad.
They point their rifles.
They lower them.

The condemned man
Falls and gets up,
Falls and gets up.
He wears a plastic blindfold.

The china doll gravediggers
Don't work so well.
The spades are too heavy.
The spades are much too heavy.

Perhaps, that's how
It's supposed to be.

GREEN LAMPSHADE

All the pages of all the books
are blank.
It's a big secret.
The readers say nothing about it
to each other.

On my block
every house is a library.
There are lights.
Late into the night
severe women
enforce complete silence.

I've been reading so much
my eyes hurt.
It's a book on astronomy,
or perhaps a book on the architecture
of prisons.

Across,
the free thinker's taking notes
furiously.
At the exit,
my father's checking out
a little volume
the size of a breviary.

I know I'm much older than he.
I have grey hairs,
wear a shabby overcoat,
will lick my forefinger
before I turn
the next page.

MY WIDOW

A photograph of a woman in black.
I cut her out of a history book.
I talk to her like a lover.
I want to cheer her up.

I set our supper table.
I turn the lights on when the evening comes.
When I turn them off,
I can hear her sigh.

She comes from Poznan.
One of her feet is shorter than the other.
She studied French in school.
She can still recite a bit of Villon.

Now she's walking through the snow.
She's coming my way,
But there's a wolf-headed dog behind her,
And a soldier with high squeaky boots.

A SUITCASE STRAPPED WITH A ROPE

for Jim

They made themselves so small
They could all fit in a suitcase.
The suitcase they kept under the bed,
And the bed near the open window.

They just huddled there in the dark
While the mother called out the names
To make sure no one was missing.
Her voice made them so warm, made them so sleepy.

He wanted to go out and play.
He even said so once or twice.
They told him to be quiet.
Just now the suitcase was moving.

Soon the border guards were going
To open it up,
Unless of course it was a thief
And he had another way to go.

A THEORY

If a cuckoo comes into the village
Of cuckoos to cuckoo and it's Monday,
And all the cuckoos should be outdoors working,
But instead there's no one anywhere

At home, or on the road overgrown with weeds,
Or even at the little grey schoolhouse,
Oh then, the cuckoo who came to the village
Of cuckoos to cuckoo must cuckoo alone.

VERMIN

After much thought
Much tossing and turning in the dark
They concluded
That they have no souls

Hands and feet—yes
Even a heart
Exactly where it's supposed to be
But little else
To sit down and eat with
To light the lamp for

Identical figures
In shabby overcoats
Their faces to the wall
The whitewashed wall
Of some night shelter
Some soup kitchen

No souls but plenty of vermin
A world
Where only their faint rustle
Is audible

Identical figures
With raised collars
Growing long fingernails
To surprise them

WHISPERS IN THE NEXT ROOM

The hospital barber, for example,
Who shaves the stroke victims,
Shaves lunatics in strait-jackets,
Doesn't even provide a mirror,

Is a widower, has a dog waiting
At home, a canary from a dimestore . . .
Eats beans cold from a can,
Then scrapes the bottom with his spoon . . .

Says: No one has seen me today,
Oh Lord, as I too have seen
No one, not even myself,
Bent as I was, intently, over the razor.

OVERCOAT

Big enough for the five of us
To put on
At the same time.
Bulky, but we manage

Our exit. Mr. Landlord,
We only require someone to button it
For the funeral, to let it open
For the wake.

Five hands out of a single sleeve,
In each a beer bottle
Raised in a toast
Under the bare and twisted coat-tree.

III

SHIRT

To get into it
As it lies
Crumpled on the floor
Without disturbing a single crease

Respectful
Of the way I threw it down
Last night
The way it happened to land

Almost managing
The impossible contortions
Doubling back now
Through a knotted sleeve

NAVIGATOR

I summoned Christopher Columbus.
At four in the morning
He came out of the gloom
Looking a little like my father.

On this particular voyage
He discovered nothing.
The ocean I gave him was endless,
And the ship—an open suitcase.

He was already lost.
I had forgotten to provide the stars.
Sitting with a bottle of wine in his hand,
He sung a song from his childhood.

In the song the day was breaking.
A barefoot girl
Stepped over the wet grass
To pick a sprig of mint.

And then nothing—
Only the wind rushing off with a high screech
As if it just remembered,
Where it's going, where it's been.

THE STREAM

for Russ Banks

The ear threading
the eye

all night long
the ear
on a long errand
for the eye

through the thickening
pine
white birch
over no man's land

pebbles
is it
compact in their anonymity
their gravity

accidents of location
abstract necessity

water
which takes such pains
to convince me
it is flowing

*

Summoning me
to be
two places at once

to drift
the length
of its chill
its ache

hand white
at the knuckles

live bait
the old hide and seek
in and out
of the swirl

luminous verb
carnivorous verb
innocent as sand
under its blows

                    *

An insomnia as big
as the stars'

always
on the brink—
as it were
of some deeper utterance

some harsher
reckoning

at daybreak

lightly
oh so lightly
when she brushes
against me

and the hems of her long skirt
go trailing

a bit longer

*

Nothing
that comes to nothing
for company

comes the way a hurt
the way a thought
comes

comes and keeps coming

all night meditating
on what she asks of me
when she doesn't

when I hear myself say
she doesn't

FURNITURE MOVER

Ah the great
   the venerable
whoever he is

   ahead of me
huge load
   terrific backache

   wherever
a chair's waiting
   meadow
sky
   beckoning

he is the one
   that's been
there
   without instructions
and for no wages

   a huge load
on his back
   and under his arm
thus
   always

   all in place
perfect
   just as it was
sweet home

   at the address
I never even dreamed of
   the address
I'm already changing

in a hurry
to overtake him
   to arrive
not ahead

   but just as
he sets down
   the table
the thousand·year-old
   bread crumbs

   I used to
claim
   I was part
of his load

   high up there
roped safely
   with the junk
the eviction notices

   I used to
prophesy
   he'll stumble
by and by

   No luck—
oh
   Mr. Furniture Mover
on my knees

   let me come
for once
   early
to where it's vacant

you still
on the stairs
   wheezing
between floors

and me behind the door
   in the gloom
I think I would
   let you do

what you must

DITTY

Could you live in the middle of
nowhere Virginia
could you live as in the game
of tag

live as a bride of no one
the sister of algebra
could you love and remember
and remember only to forget
could you live as a dog without a master

and you do of course you do
with the river the wind and the evening star
your little insomnia their big insomnia
each night clenching your eyes hard
clenching them with a sigh

Could you live knowing nothing
of why and where and how
live as a balmy day in dead winter
live as the kitchen radio
blaring all the sad old lyrics

and you do sweetheart you do

ELEGY

Note
as it gets darker
   that little
can be ascertained
of the particulars
   and of their true
magnitudes

note
the increasing
   unreliability
of vision
though one thing may appear
   more or less
familiar
   than another

disengaged
from reference
as they are
   in the deepening
gloom

nothing to do
but sit
   and abide
depending on memory
to provide

the vague outline
the theory
of where we are
tonight

and why
we can see
so little
    of each other
and soon
    will be
even less
    able

    in this starless
summer night
    windy and cold

    at the table
brought out
    hours ago
under a huge ash tree

    two chairs
two ambiguous figures
    each one relying
on the other
to remain faithful
    now
that one can leave
    without the other one
    knowing

    this late
in what only recently was
    a garden
a festive occasion
    elaborately planned
for two lovers

45

in the open air
at the end
of a dead-end
road
rarely traveled

o love

THE GUEST

Would he be the one,
Oh child,
Awake in a strange room
After a long afternoon sleep,

The one trying to remember
How he got there,
What he did before he went to bed,
The manner in which he closed his eyes . . .

Asking himself,
Was it the wind,
Raindrops on the windowpane,
A dream of footsteps close by . . .

Was it the silence
That made him awake
Cold and so afraid?

*

No other life. The hour when the train
Would pass. The little station of the half-
Open eye. Black and blue rails
In the chill of the heart, the marrow.

The mute whitewashed walls of the waiting room.
A bench to stretch out,
To make oneself inconspicuous,
To exist almost without an image.

A shadow-puppet—all right!
Without being seen by anyone,
For the duration of the world
Without being heard.

*

No one at all. An eye in a world
That would otherwise remain dark.
Improbable sky. His two hands.
The austere exhibits of his two hands.

They are not there. No matter. Voices
Of children on the street. Distant.
Games of another country, another age.
A hush. Breeze at the end

Of a long hot dusk. Voices. Purple clouds
That must be hurrying over the rooftops.
No one at all. Grimy pillow.
The lamps lit by the stooped widows.

*

Things and their shadows.
Their vast powers of persuasion.
It is still light outside.
The breeze parting the curtains.

The house by the river, for instance.
This house seen from a great distance
With its dark windows
Toward which the guest travels.

A deadman's hat raised in greeting.
Further on a door opening.
Empty sky.
A nightbird indigenous to these regions.

NOTE SLIPPED UNDER A DOOR

I saw a high window struck blind
By the late afternoon sunlight.

I saw a towel
With many dark fingerprints
Hanging in the kitchen.

I saw an old apple tree,
A shawl of wind over its shoulders,
Inch its lonely way
Toward the barren hills.

I saw an unmade bed
And felt the cold of its sheets.

I saw a fly soaked in pitch
Of the coming night
Watching me because it couldn't get out.

I saw stones that had come
From a great purple distance
Huddle around the front door.

DECEMBER TREES

Dark wood, I give myself entirely over
To your craftsmen. In a clearing,
They sized me up and then took their distance.
Quiet folk, bent, emaciated,

For such is the season. Without clues,
With hands raised, I stood like a mare
In a blacksmith's shop. Smoke
Of a late December sunlight . . .

Soft bellows of approaching dusk,
As the birches put on their heavy aprons
And reached among the branches for irons,
They hid there, so long, with leaves on.

GROCERY

Figure or figures unknown
Keep a store
Keep it open
Nights and all day Sunday

Half of what they sell
Will kill you
The other half
Makes you go back for more

Too cheap to turn on the lights
Hard to tell what it is
They've got on the counter
What it is you're paying for

All the rigors
All the solemnities
Of a brass scale imperceptibly quivering
In the early winter dusk

One of its pans
For their innards
The other one for yours—
And yours heavier

CLASSIC BALLROOM DANCES

Grandmothers who wring the necks
Of chickens; old nuns
With names like Theresa, Marianne,
Who pull schoolboys by the ear;

The intricate steps of pickpockets
Working the crowd of the curious
At the scene of an accident; the slow shuffle
Of the evangelist with a sandwich-board;

The hesitation of the early morning customer
Peeking through the window-grille
Of a pawnshop; the weave of a little kid
Who is walking to school with eyes closed;

And the ancient lovers, cheek to cheek,
On the dancefloor of the Union Hall,
Where they also hold charity raffles
On rainy Monday nights of an eternal November.

MY LITTLE UTOPIA

No one's quite sure
Why they keep it locked
At night, but they do,
Punctually. At seven

The old night-watchman
Shuffles by yelling
For the wolf and the lamb
To stop grazing.

There are none,
But he yells anyway,
As he fusses,
As he locks the heavy gate . . .

I think it's because
Of the classy fence,
The high, wrought-iron fence
With silver spikes.

HARSH CLIMATE

The brain itself in its skull
Is very cold,
According to
Albertus Magnus.

Something like a stretch of tundra
On the scale of the universe.
Galactic wind.
Lofty icebergs in the distance.

Polar night.
A large ocean liner caught in the ice.
A few lights still burning on the deck.
Silence and fierce cold.

PEACEFUL KINGDOM

The bird who watches me
sleeping
from the branch of an apple tree
in bloom.

A black bird
for whom a strange man
gathers rocks
in the ruts of the road.

*

And among the willow trees:
water
before water made up its mind
to be water.

My sister says if I drink
of that water I will die . . .
That's why the heart beats:
to waken the water.

BEDTIME STORY

When a tree falls in a forest
And there's no one around
To hear the sound, the poor owls
Have to do all the thinking.

They think so hard they fall off
Their perch and are eaten by ants,
Who, as you already know, all look like
Little Black Riding Hoods.

NOWHERE

That's where No lives,
Happily ever after.

Its sky has no stars,
No morning or evening,
No earth under its feet.

It's happy because
It only has a word for them,
And the poor Yes
Has a place,

Has a kitchen and a window
To go along with the place,
And an onion
That makes him cry.

IV

THE TOMB OF STÉPHANE MALLARMÉ

Beginning to know
  how the die
navigates
  how it makes
its fateful decisions
  in eternal circumstances
what it feels like
  to be held tight
between the thumb
  and the forefinger
to be hexed
  and prayed over
to wake up lucid
  at the heart of the shipwreck
a dark pilot's cabin
  of the die on the move
to have the earth and heaven
  repeatedly reversed
to have the mirror and the razor
  momentarily aligned
only to fall
  head over heels
to be set adrift
  in the middle of
nowhere

  the die
worn clean
  by endless conjectures
my die
  perfectly illegible
white
  as a milk tooth
the perfect die
  rolling

picking up speed
   how delightful
this new contingency
   occupancy
both inside and outside
   the unthinkable

the blindman's die
   free of
the divinatory urge
   the Number
even if it existed
   the death-defying
somersault
   beating the supreme odds
two by two
   along for the ride
only
   the roller-coaster
endlessly changing directions
   and mind
in a state of blessed
   uncertainty

cast
   on the great improbable
table
   among the ghostly salt-cellars
bones
   breadcrumbs that say
there goes:
   Cerberus' new toy
Death's great amateur
   night
the childhood of Parmenides

oh yeah

LIKE WHIPPOORWILLS

It–it–it!
That's what the strange bird said,

and another answered,
likewise,

without identifying the agent,
some animal or thing.

Very thoughtful of them,
I'm sure.

*

With the woods so thick and murky,
poor so and so . . .

A frailest twig,
and then the tip of that twig
for a soapbox,

explaining:

it looks like it,
and it acts like it,
but who's to say?

*

That it has a wish,
that it has a wishbone,

deep, deep
in their throats,

which is why
they are here this evening,

in the vicinity of,
in the dizzying nearness of,

which is why they proclaim
that it is so.

*

The place of wonder.

I often wondered what
it would be like?

Their woods hung with black crepe.
Their sky playing with matches.

Fortune's told
on the giddiest branches:

Odd fortune added
oddly.

Harken to be sure.

*

By eaves and leaves.

How like leave-
taking.

How like St. Francis
saying:

little brother,
little sister.

Last half-note,
half-twig.

I'm very anxious,
they're very anxious

to have it be
thus.